0 1341 0817698 0

MW01122444

The Trials of
John Demjanjuk

A Holocaust
Cabaret

The Trials of John Demjanjuk

A Holocaust Cabaret

Jonathan Garfinkel

Music by Christine Brubaker & Allen Cole

Playwrights Canada Press
Toronto • Canada

Playwrights Canada Press
The Canadian Drama Publisher
215 Spadina Avenue, Suite 230, Toronto, Ontario CANADA M5T 2C7
416-703-0013 fax 416-408-3402
orders@playwrightscanada.com • www.playwrightscanada.com

Financial support provided by the taxpayers of Canada and Ontario through the Canada Council for the Arts and the Department of Canadian Heritage through the Book Publishing Industry Development Programme, and the Ontario Arts Council.

Front cover photo of Christine Brubaker by Andjelija Djuric.
Production Editor/Cover design: JLArt

Library and Archives Canada Cataloguing in Publication

Garfinkel, Jonathan
    The trials of John Demjanjuk : a Holocaust cabaret / Jonathan Garfinkel ; music by Christine Brubaker & Allen Cole.

A play.
ISBN 0-88754-774-5

    1. Demjanjuk, John--Trials, litigation, etc.--Drama. 2. War crime trials--Israel--Drama. 3. Treblinka (Concentration camp)--Drama. I. Cole, Allen II. Brubaker, Christine III. Title.

PS8563.A646T75 2005   C812'.6   C2005-904170-6

First edition: July 2005.
Printed and bound by AGMV Marquis at Quebec, Canada.

"Two souls, alas, reside within my breast
And each withdraws from and repels its brother."
                                            —Goethe

The Trials of John Demjanjuk: An Introduction

by Vivian Rakoff

Jonathan Garfinkel has written a brave play. This isn't a tactful way of saying foolhardy, tactless, unaware, grandiose or any other such thing. He is clearly aware that the Shoah is both forbidding and almost forbidden as a literary topic let alone a comedy, and what's more, a cabaret comedy—that most secular, frivolous genre. It has been said that the Holocaust demands silence, contemplation, respect—and that after the Holocaust no poetry can be written. But the challenge to understand it—even to consider it remains. Any writing about the Shoah is shadowed by a massive dramatic irony. We "all know what happened" (apart from Holocaust deniers) and that knowledge can render any fictionalising trivial or indeed blasphemous. The inescapable fact of the Holocaust is simply THERE!—a mountain of smoky darkness. The usual techniques of making art out of experience are inadequate. It cannot be shown directly; it is blinding and bewildering. What come to mind are the devices people use to observe an eclipse of the sun: to gaze at it directly involves the risk of burning the retina, indelibly scarring it, or blindness. For many of us it is in the category of the unapproachably sacred—a desolate holy of holies.

But the fact is the Holocaust as topic is not sealed up in some sacred vault. It is very much in the secular arena and as one of the characters in *The Trials of John Demjanjuk* says, "There's no business like Shoah business," giving voice to the discomfort caused by exploitative sentimentalising which frivolously hijacks the tragedy. The topic has become like a disputed piece of real estate with attendant claims of "ownership " like the dispute surrounding "voice appropriation." One remembers the criticisms directed at *Sophie's Choice* with the not-so-subtle implication that Styron, a gentile, should not be writing about a Jewish concentration camp experience.

Direct depiction of the Holocaust is for historians and eye witnesses. They have an implicit right; more than that an intellectual and moral duty to preserve the horrors for posterity. They are the guardians against forgetting. But for the writer of fiction, indirection seems to be the only possible literary stance. And there are some examples which already represent a daunting canon of high achievement for a novice trying to grapple with the topic: In *Sophie's*

Choice, although Styron tells a Holocaust story, his sense of tentative awe for the topic shows in the complicated nuances of the plot; a kind of glancing sideways look. Even Eli Wiesel's *Night*—one of the earliest "literary" documents of the Holocaust literature canon, for all its spare journalistic style, an apparently unadorned reporting, is a child's story, an exercise in meiosis in which the huge events are seen in microcosm. In the allusive flickering poems of Paul Celan, metaphor, mournful veiling and obscurity convey the essential incomprehensibility of his experience. And in the magisterial succession of Aharon Apelfeld's short novels, the Holocaust is, in the classical Greek sense "obscene"; too terrible to be represented mimetically. In *Badenheim* the murders and deportations are played out diminuendo by animals, a resort orchestra, ordinary silly people at a spa, or in his other novels in which the Holocaust is in the future or in the past.

Garfinkel's play with its distancing devices of song, caricature and clowning is in an honourable tradition. He avoids the sentimentality of "Life is Beautiful" which adds nothing to understanding and substitutes denial for despair and humiliation. Garfinkel looks for truths and examines complex events using the licence of the classical clown who plays white-faced, red-nosed and a painted death's head grin, the inevitable falling down towards death. Or the fool or court jester who was allowed to say things in the mitigating capsule of the humourous... "It was only a joke." He understands that being funny may be one of the bearable ways to speak of the unspeakable. The best jokes are about the most difficult topics—sex, death and money. And humour in good taste may be an oxymoron. In the theatre it helps us endure the unendurable.

For all its theatrical verve *The Trials of John Demjanjuk* touches on complexity. Although it deals in caricature, Demjanjuk is not a caricature. Garfinkel humanises him, he forces us to face his ordinariness; he is not a de-humanised monster but a factory worker who goes to a baseball game with his son. An act of literary charity of more depth than one would expect in a short, stylised play. He also pays a complex homage to the Israeli Justice system. In spite of Demjanjuk's trial being a "show trial," his defence lawyer energetically, angrily and cynically gives him his full day in court and obtains his release. Against the understandable fury and the understandable desire for vengeance of survivors, Demjanjuk benefits from civilised doubt and the ideals of rule of law. He is a Shylock among the vengeance seeking Venetians who is allowed to go free.

I've put Garfinkel's cabaret piece into some impressive company. Although it doesn't have the grandeur of the works I've briefly mentioned it has loads of the necessary virtue of a piece for the theatre; it entertains while it appalls and instructs. Brecht would have been proud of such an apt pupil.

Author's Notes

This work blurs the boundaries between fiction and non-fiction. I have remained faithful to actual courtroom events, compressing them to fit the temporal needs of the theatre. The prosecution and defense scenes contain direct quotes from trial transcripts. Scene fifteen contains direct quotes taken from the testimony of the survivor Czarny. The line, "There's no business like Shoah business" was originally coined by Abba Eban, former Israeli foreign minister. All flashbacks, interactions between John and Ivan, and scenes outside the court of law are from the author's imagination.

I would like to thank Adam Sol, who read the poem version of this and said it was wanting to be a play. Thanks also to John Murrell, Alex Poch-Goldin, Gadi Roll, Jason Sherman, Paul Thompson and Kelly Thornton for their invaluable insights at various stages of the play's development. Thanks to The Banff playRites Colony, Lise Anne Johnson and the NAC, Marc Glassman, Mitch Smolkin and the Ashkenaz Festival, and Buddies in Bad Times Theatre. Thanks to all of the actors in all the workshops and productions, whose feedback and enthusiasm helped push this play past its original skin. To Christine Brubaker, Dmitry Chepovetsky and Clinton Walker for their commitment to *The Trials* over the years, and to Christine for scoring the music.

Many thanks to Jennifer Herszman Capraru, who suggested the Brechtian cabaret style with scene titles, who gave birth to the character of Fraülein, and submitted this when it was still a poem to the Rhubarb! Festival. Thanks to the drunken singing of JHC, Josh Dolgin and Tobaran Waxman, which inspired the possibility of song.

The Trials of John Demjanjuk received its World Premiere at the Chutzpah Festival, Vancouver, produced by Theatre Asylum, Toronto in February 2004 with the following company:

John Demjanjuk	Frank Moore
Ivan the Terrible	Dmitry Chepovetsky
Fraülein/Mama	Christine Brubaker
Rosie/The Survivor/Mordecai	Clinton Walker
Shaked/Nazi 1/Sher	Michael Rubenfeld
Sheftel/Nazi 2/Russek	Dov Mickelson

Directed and dramaturged by Jennifer H. Capraru
Lighting by Sandra Marcroft
Set and Costumes by Andjelija Djuric
Sound design by E.C. Woodley
Stage manager: Andrew Dollar

It was also performed with the same company at Intrepid Theatre, Victoria in February 2004 and Harbourfront Studio Theatre, Toronto in March 2004 as part of the HATCH Festival.

•••

The Trials of John Demjanjuk: A Holocaust Cabaret was workshopped at the Banff playRites Colony 2003—a partnership between the Canada Council for the Arts, the Banff Centre for the Arts, and Alberta Theatre Projects.

The Trials of John Demjanjuk: A Holocaust Cabaret had two workshop productions by Theatre Asylum in Toronto. It was performed at Rhubarb Festival, February 2002 at Buddies in Bad Times Theatre.

The Trials was invited to the Ashkenaz Festival of New Yiddish Culture at Harbourfront, September 2002, where it was performed in a sixty-minute version.

The Trials was also workshopped and received a public reading as part of the National Arts Centre's English Theatre On the Verge Theatre New Works Festival 2003.

Characters

Das Fraülein	Accordion-playing German cabaret narrator and temptress
Rosie	Fraülein's sidekick
Yoram Sheftel	Defense Attorney, late 30s
Michael Shaked	Prosecuting Attorney, early 30s
Mr. Russek	Head of Israeli War Crimes Unit
Mr. Sher	Head of Office of Special Investigations
John Jr.	John's 12-year-old son
John Demjanjuk	67, Ukrainian
Ivan the Terrible	Mid 20s, Ukrainian
The Survivor	60s
Mama	John's mother
Mordecai	Communist Jew, 20s
Nazi 1 & 2	Two cartoonish dimwits of any age

Clinton Walker, Michael Rubenfeld, Frank Moore,
Dmitry Chepovetsky, Dov Mickelson
photo by Jonathan Garfinkel

THE TRIALS OF JOHN DEMJANJUK
A HOLOCAUST CABARET

PROLOGUE

"The Ballad of John Demjanjuk"

FRAÜLEIN   There once was a man
    named John Demjanjuk
    They said he was Ivan
    that terrible prep-line cook

    Who sent off the Jews
    to bake and to rise
    And smeared their black breath
    in the blue Polish skies

    The place was Treblinka
    where the summers were hot
    Kurt Franz and Stangl
    were the big shots

    They had dreams of a golf course,
    a garden, a zoo
    And they employed Germans,
    Ukrainians and Jews

    It was there they made lampshades
    and the gold supply grew
    They served near one million
    before the first year was through

    And though the skies were still hungry
    there were no more Jews

ROSIE   Except for the fifty
    who escaped through the fields

Clinton Walker, Christine Brubaker
photo by Andjelija Djuric

Now I know about Ivan
his scar and his scowl
The lead pipe he carried
made the kids howl

He ran the gas chambers
vodka his muse
And his face was that
of a young Demjanjuk

FRAÜLEIN   In an Israeli courtroom
two lawyers stand grim
It's 1987
and the prosecution wants him

SHAKED   John Demjanjuk
must be punished and tried
It's justice we want
we say he must die

SHEFTEL   My name is Yoram Sheftel
and I drive a white Porsche
I'm Israel's top
defending lawyer of course

And the people ask why
I rose to defend
I'm an Israeli
and I'll fight to the end

SHAKED   What has happened to John
SHEFTEL   shows what can go wrong
ROSIE   when a people are angry
ALL   and want their revenge

FRAÜLEIN   These are the trials of John Demjanjuk.
    (*speaking*) Welcome. To our Cabaret of Life

ROSIE   and Death.

FRAÜLEIN   Tonight is a night of nightmares

ROSIE   and paperclips.

FRAÜLEIN   Secrets spoken.
Shocking revelations revealed.
The horrors of the human condition exposed.

ROSIE   Thrills and chills,

FRAÜLEIN   Truth—

ROSIE   and lies.

FRAÜLEIN   Tonight we present our Holocaust Cabaret.
So you came for some fun, *naja? (a beat)*
Why don't Jewish cannibals eat Germans?

ROSIE   Because it gives them gas.

FRAÜLEIN   So you came to laugh.
Or not.
To forget your problems.
To watch the torments of another man.
Thank God it is not me, you will say.
Thank God it is a monster.
This is not my story.
This is not me.

ROSIE   *Eins*—

FRAÜLEIN   How can one of the nicest men you'd ever want to
meet also be a sadistic murderer?

ROSIE   *Zwei*—

FRAÜLEIN   Is he in fact a sadistic murderer?

ROSIE   *Drei*—

FRAÜLEIN   Or is this just... a show-trial?

Scene 1

FRAÜLEIN   Washington. 1976. Voices behind closed doors.

ROSIE   Sunglasses.

FRAÜLEIN   Trenchcoats!
Mr. Russek:

ROSIE   a bold moustache.

FRAÜLEIN   A Russian nose. The head of war crimes in Israel—
(points to RUSSEK) visits Mr. Sher:

ROSIE   A very crafty

FRAÜLEIN   intelligent American

ROSIE   Head of the OSI—

FRAÜLEIN   Office of Special Investigations—

TOGETHER   the American Nazi hunters— *(points to SHER)*

> *SHEFTEL plays RUSSEK, SHAKED plays SHER. They speak spy-ishly.*

RUSSEK   We need to talk.

SHER   *(motions to walls, whispers)* We must talk quietly.

RUSSEK   *(whisper)* I have come a long way for your help.

SHER   I know. We need your help too.

RUSSEK   I need… *(whisper)* a *donut.*

SHER   A what?

RUSSEK   Last time, we had a braided vanilla… *(short pause)* donut.
Hmm? The Germanic cruller type.

SHER Uh-huh.

RUSSEK But we don't want to have to kidnap this... *donut*.

SHER I'm sorry Mr. Russek. We're not familiar with this code in Washington.

RUSSEK We. The War Crimes Unit of Israel. Have not had... a good... *DONUT* in twenty years. (*motions a Seig Heil several times*)

SHER Ahhhh. I see.

RUSSEK Your country has let dozens go through its hands uneaten.

SHER We need survivors, witnesses, evidence. Be patient.

RUSSEK Patience leads to... *donuts* running away to Argentina or the Bahamas.

SHER What are you implying?

RUSSEK If you give us one, I will ensure it gets eaten in Jerusalem.

SHER Really.

RUSSEK But it has to be... clear cut. Open and shut.

SHER Like Eichman—

RUSSEK Shhhhh! Now, we're hungry for a... *donut*, but we have to be sure it's a murderous *donut*.

SHER Which... *donut*... do you have in mind?

RUSSEK Good, Mr. Sher, very good. I hear they make excellent donuts in Cleveland. A soft—

SHER Ukrainian—

TOGETHER jelly donut.

Michael Rubenfeld, Frank Moore, Dov Mickelson
photo by Jonathan Garfinkel

SCENE 2

FRAÜLEIN   Meanwhile, at the very same moment in Cleveland—

ROSIE   fifty-thousand screaming fans!

FRAÜLEIN   Hot dogs!

ROSIE   Popcorn!

FRAÜLEIN   A baseball game. A father. A son.

JOHN JR.   (*to game*) Seaver, you're a bum!

JOHN   Are we still losing?

JOHN JR.   Yes, Dad. Just look at the scoreboard. (*groans*) That's ten strikeouts. They're gonna cream us.

JOHN   You take it so seriously.

JOHN JR.   It's do or die, Dad. The Indians haven't been in the Series since '54.

JOHN   Why does the pitcher always scratch himself like this? Is it part of the game?

JOHN JR.   Yes.

JOHN   Does he get a point for scratching himself?

JOHN JR.   No. It's just the way they do things. Shut up and watch the game.

JOHN   Look at the way the man holds his bat. Such strength. You see, Junior? To succeed, you have to be strong.

JOHN JR.   Do you always have to talk like everything is some kind of lesson? (*to game*) Come on, ya bum. Keep your eye on the ball! Strike one. You can do it! Strike two. The pitch. A hit. He hit it!

JOHN   Hard.

JOHN JR.   It could go.

JOHN   It's going—

JOHN JR.   It's going—

JOHN   It's gone.

JOHN JR.   Home run, Dad. Off Seaver!

JOHN   He did it.

JOHN JR.   It was impossible.

JOHN   No son. It's not impossible. It's America.

SCENE 3

"John was a Regular Fella"

FRAÜLEIN   (*singing*) It was a bright and sunny
          Cleveland day
          The elm trees sighed,
          life was gay

          John was tired
          needed to rest his feet
          His work was over
          Goodbye to the week

          Neighbours' voices: a chorus.

VOICES   John was a regular fella
          He worked in his garden
          He played with the kids
          He liked to get his hands dirty

He fit in well with our
Ohio digs

FRAÜLEIN   John did not believe
the noises he heard
His quiet home
had become a circus of the absurd

A camera flash
click click and dash
What's going on
to poor old John?

> *The sound of cameras. JOHN is bombarded by reporters
> speaking.*

REPORTER 1   Mr. Demjanjuk, what do you have to say about the
accusations?
REPORTER 2   Is your wife upset?
REPORTER 3   Did you really enjoy gassing Jews?

CHORUS   John was a regular fella
He worked in the garden
He played with the kids
He liked to get his hands dirty
He fits in well with our
Ohio digs

> *Speaking.*

REPORTER 1   Is it true you were a POW?
REPORTER 2   Do you have a criminal record?
REPORTER 3   Did you know that the OSI has been tracking you for
three years?
REPORTER 1   What do you have to say to the public?
REPORTER 2   Your neighbours
REPORTER 3   your children
REPORTER 1   your church
REPORTER 2   your mother

FRAÜLEIN   your wife?
(*singing*) John says nothing

What's there to say?
Vera faints in his arms
and she's carried away

JOHN   (*speaking*) My poor Vera.
Frail, white Vera.
These are my tears
on your neck.

What are they doing to us?

Scene 4

FRAÜLEIN   Jerusalem is a passionate place.
Prime Minister Shamir has just promised to crush the Palestinians
like grasshoppers.
The first Intifadah has begun.

ROSIE   That's not what we're talking about tonight.

FRAÜLEIN   I smell blood.

ROSIE   Fresh blood.

FRAÜLEIN   John is nervous.

ROSIE   Terrified.

FRAÜLEIN   Life

ROSIE   or death. (*They laugh somewhat hysterically.*)

FRAÜLEIN   1976.

ROSIE   Survivors identify Demjanjuk as Ivan of Treblinka.

FRAÜLEIN   1978.

ROSIE   John's family goes on a hunger strike

Clinton Walker
photo by Andjelija Djuric

FRAÜLEIN   1981.

ROSIE   John's American citizenship is revoked.

FRAÜLEIN   1985.

ROSIE   John is thrown into a Cleveland jail.

FRAÜLEIN   1986.

ROSIE   John is deported to Israel.

FRAÜLEIN   The long-awaited trial...
Begins NOW.
The star of our show.
Alone in the Promised Land

ROSIE   They promised us the trial would be short.

FRAÜLEIN   But it wasn't.
John sits in the court and watches.

ROSIE   The audience watches him.

FRAÜLEIN   The accused takes the stand!

JOHN   In 1952
I entered the United States

And though I left out a few irrelevant details about my past
I received my certificate of Naturalisation
I have the number
to prove it

It was different in those days
Fighting in Ukraine in the war
Who knew what we were doing

When the Nazis caught me
I walked through it all in a fever
In 1942-43

I was a POW in Chelm
Mourning for my dead father

I never lied
except during the first immigration hearing
When I said I was a farmer in Sobibor
it was to protect my wife
I didn't know it was a death camp
Never heard of the place
Saw it once on a map

As for the tattoo
under my armpit
the SS put it there
In the Displaced Persons camp
I rubbed it out with a stone
I thought it might be taken
the wrong way

       Various voices whisper/echo JOHN.

JOHN   I was starved

ROSIE   *starved*

JOHN   beaten

ROSIE   *beaten*

JOHN   I forgot everything
           I was dead to myself
           Only the dust in my throat
           reminded me I had breath

ROSIE   *Breath*

JOHN   But I'm innocent

EVERYONE   *innocent*

JOHN   I am not Ivan of Treblinka.

I know it.
My hands
they're twitching
with the truth

EVERYONE   *truth*

Scene 5

FRAÜLEIN   There is fear in this theatre.
People are fainting.
Loved ones are crying.

ROSIE   Everyone is afraid to remember.

FRAÜLEIN   But who is telling the truth?

Our young *ünd* dashing prosecutor, Michael Shaked, wants to see
the defendant dead. All rise in the court of law!

SHAKED   We are the children of Auschwitz. Majdanek. And
Treblinka. Our country has been born from the smoke of such
terrible fathers and mothers.

Eleven years ago, survivors in Tel Aviv and New York were
shown a series of photographs, a "photospread." Without being
prompted, several of these eyewitnesses positively identified John
Demjanjuk as Ivan the Terrible of Treblinka. How is this possible?
The horror which marked the lives of the survivors will never
allow them to forget. No matter how many years pass, their
memories remain clear and precise.

The central evidence for our case is the Travniki identity card.
This I.D. card will prove, beyond a shadow of a doubt, that John
Demjanjuk voluntarily trained at Travniki camp to become an SS
guard, an expert in torture and extermination techniques.

In this trial, we will prove that Mr. Demjanjuk's alibi is based on
lies. That he willfully participated in the murder of nearly one

million people at Treblinka death camp. That he committed atrocities such as slicing open the bellies of pregnant women with a machete. This man, who insists on his innocence, is the embodiment of evil itself. I beg the judges to consider the evidence very carefully, and judge Demjanjuk guilty, before this court, before our nation, and before God.

Scene 6

FRAÜLEIN   Alone in his cell… John tries his best not to be afraid.

JOHN in his cell doing pushups.

JOHN   One hundred and ten. One hundred and eleven. One hundred and twelve. *(stops)* Strong body. Strong mind. Strong spirit. They think they're going to defeat me? They think I am weak?

ROSIE   *(whisper) Monster*
SHAKED   *(whisper) Murderer.*
TOGETHER   *(whisper) Death to Ivan of Treblinka*

JOHN   Isolated. Humiliated. Video surveillance. Not a second goes by without people watching me. I saw my son cry in the courtroom today. My wife Vera sends me packages that are opened before I get them. I miss conversations with her, in the middle of the night, when one of us can't sleep. Ordinary people. And below our bedroom, the ordinary streets of Seven Hills, Ohio.

VOICE 1   *Never late*
VOICE 2   *Never called in sick*
VOICE 3   *Never talked about the war*
VOICE 4   *If he's guilty they made him do it*
ALL   *And his perogies are absolutely the best!*

JOHN gets down on his knees.

JOHN   Mama

Look at your boy. I'm sixty-seven years old.
Don't let them destroy me.
I never hurt a soul.
Pray for me, Mama.

Tonight the full moon will rise. I know this because the Jews do.
Their calendar tells them so. I've begun to study their language.
Ani naki. Ani eesh shalom. I am innocent. I am a man of peace.

Scene 7

JOHN falls asleep. IVAN the Terrible appears. He sings.

"The Myth of Ivan the Terrible"

IVAN I'm Ivan the Terrible
God, what a name
I put the devil
and his angels to shame
I am here to bring out the darkness in men

If your water's too pure
Your garden too green
If your body is soft
and your mind is too clean
I'll be sure to muck it and maim it again

Oh the moon has a nice look tonight
But it's only reflection
It is not its own light
If your conscience seems a little too quiet
I have come to inspire it
To remember some things that you'd probably rather forget

Treblinka was grand
But since that great war
There's been lots to do
Thank God life's no bore
And I have many an SS to thank

Yes the moon has a nice look tonight
But it's only reflection
It is not its own light
If your conscience seems a little too quiet
I have come to inspire it
To remember some things that I'm sure that you'll never forget

SCENE 8

JOHN wakes up suddenly. He is frozen with fear.

IVAN   Achtung! Good. You're standing at attention.
You're still a soldier.

JOHN   What do you want?

IVAN   To help you.

JOHN   I don't want your help.

IVAN   You didn't fare too well up on the stand today. Very nervous.

JOHN   Wouldn't you be?

IVAN   I'm grateful to you. For bringing me into the spotlight again.
I enjoy the attention.

JOHN   I don't.

IVAN   No. You always were a shy boy. Even during the famine,
when your mother found you the meat. You didn't tell a soul.
(*pause*)

There's an old Ukrainian saying:
Speak your mind,
the truth is your gift.

JOHN   I can't remember everything.

IVAN   Just tell them the truth, John.

JOHN   There were many details. It was very long ago.

IVAN   You know who you are.
You know where you come from.

SCENE 9

FRAÜLEIN   (*whispers*) John has a flashback, just like in the movies. The hamlet of Duboviye Makharyntsy, Ukraine 1933. It's the Great Famine, compliments of Comrade Stalin. John is thirteen years old.

MAMA   Vanichka! Come and eat.

JOHN   Where did you get this meat? (*Silence. JOHN is eating.*) It tastes like heaven, Mama.

MAMA   We are harvesting the will of the Lord. He has willed that you survive.

JOHN   The meat is so tender.

MAMA   The Lord provideth.

JOHN   I feel strong already, Mama. I could go back to work in the fields, right now. (*searching, whistling*) Here, Pisha, Pisha. Hey. Where's Pisha?

MAMA   Eat. You need your food. You're a growing boy.

JOHN   I love you Mama.... Wait. Where did this meat come from? (*pause*) Mama?

MAMA   Pisha is giving you strength, John.

JOHN   What?

MAMA   There was nothing to feed him.

JOHN   You…

MAMA   Don't you dare waste it.

JOHN   Pisha is our dog. You gave him to me ten years ago.

MAMA   Your father is not to know of this. It will only make him jealous.

JOHN   Oh God.

MAMA   Do you want to be like the neighbours? Eating their dead?

JOHN   (*a beat*) Thank you, Mama. (*resumes eating*)

MAMA   Tomorrow you're going to work for Vladimir.

JOHN   Yes, Mama.

MAMA   Say grace with me. "Thank thee, O Lord, for providing us this…"

JOHN   (*aside*) Smell of bodies
rotting on the banks
Eyes of my dog
stare
wherever I turn

SCENE 10

"The Ballad of John the Good"

FRAÜLEIN   Now Johnny was a good boy
he worked in the Ukrainian fields
In the year of 1933
Stalin took all their yields

ROSIE   And the Ukrainian people starved to death
In fact seven million did die
In the empty fields where the food once grew
that's where the bodies did lie

TOGETHER   Johnny moved to a farm
where he drove a big truck
He liked to fix engines
he had the good luck

ROSIE   To be skilled as a driver
was a rare and very good thing

FRAÜLEIN   And though our Johnny he wasn't a genius

TOGETHER   The bastard could fix anything

SCENE 11

FRAÜLEIN   Yoram Sheftel, that famous defence attorney, visits John in his cell.

JOHN   How much is my family paying you?

SHEFTEL   You're getting a bargain John.

JOHN   But how can they afford it?

SHEFTEL   I'll admit, I'm not the cheapest lawyer in the business. But let's face it: without me, you don't stand a chance in hell.

JOHN   I know.

SHEFTEL   And I know what you Ukrainians did to us during the war. My grandmother told me all about it. But I've chosen to defend you anyway.

JOHN   Because we pay you a lot.

SHEFTEL   No. I don't need your money. I'm defending you because I don't trust this country. They won't give you a fair trial.

JOHN   What does this mean?

SHEFTEL   You're going to hang.

JOHN   Then what the hell are you defending me for?

SHEFTEL   Don't get excited.

JOHN   Don't you believe I'm innocent?

SHEFTEL   Of course I do.

JOHN   This is about having your name in the newspaper.

SHEFTEL   No, John. This is about you.

JOHN   (*unsure*) Uh-huh.

SHEFTEL   I'm going to do my best to save your skin. But I need your help. I need you to tell me what you really did during the war.

JOHN   I have. I told it in court. I'm an honest man.

SHEFTEL   (*a beat*) Good. Talk about your family more. We need to appeal to their sense of humanity.

Scene 12

FRAÜLEIN   A white porsche.

ROSIE   *Kapo.*

FRAÜLEIN   Love beads.

ROSIE   *Self-hating Jew.*

FRAÜLEIN   Got the gangster Meyer Lansky off the hook.
Won the Billion Shekel Robbery.
Ladies and gentlemen, bachelor #2, Yoram Sheftel,
Defence attorney, begins his… Crusade for Truth.

SHEFTEL   My dear Judges. All the questions in this case can be
reduced to one: Do we want justice, or do we want retribution?

We, the Jewish people, have spent two thousand years demanding
justice. We abhor those, like the Nazi state, who set up separate
laws against us. But are we doing anything different to this man?

My client has already been denied the basic tenets of international
law. He is guilty, waiting to be proven innocent. In this case, I will
prove that the KGB forged the "Travniki identity card." And that
the photos of suspected Nazis were biased. Through the haze of
forty-five years, the survivors chose the man whose photo was the
largest. Why? Because they want an answer. And we need an
answer.

But this former theatre is proof you did not come to give John
Demjanjuk a fair trial. You came to watch the performance of
vengeance. You bow to the TV camera, to the press, and have
decided that this man is Ivan the Terrible of Treblinka.

We all live next door to neighbours. This man who sits before
you is your neighbour. He works hard and lives an honest life.
You know his kids. You've seen him at Church or Synagogue.
Because of people like him, the world is a good place. Take
a good look at this man. And before you send him to the gallows,
be sure. This is not the face of evil.

Scene 13

FRAÜLEIN   What's the difference between a carp and a lawyer?

ROSIE   One's a bottom-feeding, scum-eating animal…

FRAÜLEIN   ...the other makes great gefilte fish.
    (*announces*) "**The Dueling Lawyers' Duet**"

SHAKED   To defend the person before you
    is to reject history's trial
    The defence's primary funder
    is a Holocaust denier

    Justice is implicit in this courtroom
    This is a righteous prosecution
    Demjanjuk's crime of genocide
    grants his guilt and execution

SHEFTEL   If it's the defence's funder you condemn
    then will you please invite him to the stand
    If it's truth and wisdom you condone
    then a fair trial I demand

SHAKED   I'll fight for the memory

SHEFTEL   I'll fight for the truth

SHAKED   I'll fight your damn ego

SHEFTEL   I'll find all the proof

SHAKED   I'll fight you until the end

SHEFTEL   I'm sharpening my claws

SHAKED   We'll meet up in this courtroom

TOGETHER   We'll see who knows the laws

SHEFTEL   Do you hear how the state beckons
    with the vengeance of the ages
    Israel listens not to reason
    and puts liberty in cages

    My dear client is a victim
    of the whims of the state

Dov Mickelson
photo by Jonathan Garfinkel

The OSI wants to indict him
and hang him for their mistakes

SHAKED   If it's truth and wisdom you condone
then please invite your client to the stand
If it's Israel that you condemn
your blindness I reprimand

SHEFTEL   I'll fight for the underdog

SHAKED   I'll fight for the truth

SHEFTEL   I'll fight this damned government

SHAKED   I'll find all the proof

SHEFTEL   I'll fight you until the end

SHAKED   I'm sharpening my claws

SHEFTEL   We'll meet up in this courtroom

SHAKED   We'll see who knows the laws

SHEFTEL   I am a proud Israeli

SHAKED   You're a Judas of Jews

SHEFTEL   Here in this televised courtroom

SHAKED   The world is watching us

SHEFTEL   We'll see which one of us

TOGETHER   We'll see which one of us will lose!

SCENE 14

FRAÜLEIN   John's cell. An Invitation.

> *JOHN alone.*

JOHN   I saw Junior.
He's too thin.
I liked Vera's blue hat.

> *IVAN appears.*

IVAN   Sentimental crap.
I watched the survivors. Their stories make me sound like a god.

JOHN   Their faces were dripping with tears.

IVAN   I wanted to kill them all.

JOHN   How can you say that?

IVAN   It's us or them, John.
Soon the court will bring the survivors to the stand.

JOHN   What will they say?

IVAN   Whatever the prosecution wants.

JOHN   What do they want?

IVAN   You.
So. Do you want my help yet?

JOHN   Do I have a choice?

SCENE 15

FRAÜLEIN   The defence calls to the stand
The Survivor
from Treblinka death camp

ROSIE becomes THE SURVIVOR.

THE SURVIVOR   In Warsaw I studied the Bible and Dostoevsky
My dream was to be a scholar
When home became a ghetto
I became the breadwinner
scavenged Dluka Street for food

The last time I saw my mother I was seventeen
On the train to Treblinka
she gave me her wedding ring
I traded the gold for bread

SHEFTEL   In 1976 you were shown a photo spread. You identified
John Demjanjuk as Ivan the Terrible.

THE SURVIVOR   Yes.

SHEFTEL   Do you remember the size of the photograph of Mr.
Demjanjuk?

THE SURVIVOR   Not exactly.

SHEFTEL   Allow me to help you remember. The picture of Mr.
Demjanjuk was twice as large as any of the others. Did you ever
think this might help influence your identification of John
Demjanjuk?

THE SURVIVOR   Certainly not. I remember what Ivan looked like.

SHEFTEL   What do you remember from Treblinka?

THE SURVIVOR   A dog, named Bari. He belonged to the
commander Kurt Franz, whom we called Lalka.

SHEFTEL   Lalka?

THE SURVIVOR   It means doll. Lalka used to set his dog Bari against us. He was trained to attack a Jew's genitals. Lalka would say to Bari, "Man, bite dog!" And the dog would attack. The man would be running with blood between his legs—

SHEFTEL   I'm sure that was a terrible thing to have witnessed.

THE SURVIVOR   You cannot imagine.

SHEFTEL   Unfortunately, this has nothing to do with our case from a legal standpoint. Sir, I need you to tell the court about the process of identifying Ivan the Terrible—

THE SURVIVOR   There he is, sitting in front of me.

SHEFTEL   How do you know?

THE SURVIVOR   Three times a day we used to pray to Jerusalem. That was our hope. Now I am in Jerusalem. But I am still in Treblinka.

SHEFTEL   We need you to be sure—

THE SURVIVOR   This man sitting before you pushed children into gas chambers with an iron pipe and a bayonet.

SHEFTEL   Sir I—

THE SURVIVOR   I never wanted my children to hear this. Do you know if my daughter is here?

SHEFTEL   Did the survivors get together in Florida to discuss this case?

THE SURVIVOR   No.

SHEFTEL   Did you discuss this case with any of the survivors before you came to court?

Dmitry Chepovetsky
photo by Jonathan Garfinkel

THE SURVIVOR   We're friends. Do you think I don't talk to these people?

SHEFTEL   Did you discuss the photo spreads?

THE SURVIVOR   Not in any way that would seem inappropriate.

SHEFTEL   So there was a group discussion?

THE SURVIVOR   We often get together. We need to talk about our experiences.

SHEFTEL   Thank you. No further questions, your honour.

SCENE 16

In the cell. JOHN is practicing for the case.

FRAÜLEIN   Lessons for Survival.

JOHN   Your honour, I worked on the Ford Assembly Line for twenty-five years.

IVAN   Louder.

JOHN   YOUR HONOUR, I WORKED ON THE FORD ASSEMBLY LINE FOR TWENTY-FIVE YEARS.

IVAN   More dignified.

JOHN   I'm a retired mechanic from the Ford Company. I worked there for twenty-five years, *sir.*

IVAN   Better. Then tell them about the engines. You were a *great* mechanic.

JOHN   I was a decent mechanic.

IVAN   You *love* engines.

JOHN   No, I like engines. When I open the hood of my truck, I look inside, I feel there's an order to things, the world can be understood.

IVAN   Good. So what does your truck run on?

JOHN   Diesel.

IVAN   Why?

JOHN   Cheaper fuel.

IVAN   More efficient.

JOHN   Diesel doesn't break down as much.

IVAN   The fuel injector of a diesel engine is beautiful.

JOHN   No. Reliable.

IVAN   A work of genius.

JOHN   Practical. The fuel injector can withstand incredible amounts of heat and still deliver fuel in a fine mist. And it's not exposed like the internal combustion engine.

IVAN   But diesel's more expensive.

JOHN   Not in the long run.

IVAN   You save on gas.

JOHN   And maintenance.

IVAN   Diesel has less horsepower.

JOHN   Higher torque.

IVAN   It's slower.

JOHN   Who needs to rush? Life is a marathon—

IVAN   not a sprint. You love your diesel truck.

JOHN   I love my wife.

IVAN   You appreciate it.

JOHN   I like to fix the problems. To get in there, and work with my hands. It brings me peace.

IVAN   Me too, Vanichka. Now. Let's start again.

SCENE 17

In the court.

FRAÜLEIN   Today in court, Shaked is wearing a very tight suit. The prosecution sharpens its claws.

JOHN   I'm a retired auto mechanic from the Ford company. I worked there for twenty-five years, *sir*.

SHAKED   When did you learn how to drive a truck?

JOHN   1947.

SHAKED   Your visa states you drove for the U.S. Army at a DP camp starting from 1945.

JOHN   It's not true.

SHAKED   So you lied on your entry form?

JOHN   They must have misunderstood me. I told them I only knew how to drive a tractor.

SHAKED   And fix it?

JOHN   Yes. But to drive a truck one needed seven grades schooling, and I only had four.

SHAKED   Mr. Fedorenko was a truck driver during the war.

SHEFTEL   Objection! My client is not Fedorenko.

FRAÜLEIN   Overruled.

SHAKED   As a prisoner at Chelm, Mr. Fedorenko's life was saved because of his skills, and he became a driver at Treblinka.

JOHN   I am not Fedorenko.

SHAKED   No. But with only three years schooling he was a driver. (*pause*) At Chelm, the Germans asked all drivers to step forward. You volunteered to do so and you saved your life.

JOHN   I knew nothing about trucks.

SHAKED   You did. This is why your drivers license in 1948 said: Skilled Driver. You were a mechanic and driver during the war.

JOHN   Never.

SHAKED   Mr. Demjanjuk, you are accused of operating the gas chambers in Treblinka. Do you know that Jews were gassed in Treblinka not with Zyklon B, but by carbon monoxide from running a diesel engine?

JOHN   Yes.

SHAKED   And Ivan's duty was to maintain the diesel engine?

JOHN   Yes.

SHAKED   You admit that you knew how to fix engines before the war. The Trawniki I.D. card says you were trained as an SS guard—

SHEFTEL   Objection! The Trawniki card has not been proven authentic.

FRAÜLEIN   Sustained.

Michael Rubenfeld
photo by Jonathan Garfinkel

SHAKED   Yes, the Trawniki card which would allow a mechanic to operate the engine that killed two thousand Jews daily in Treblinka has not been proven authentic. I agree.

JOHN   The gas chamber was diesel. A tractor runs on gasoline.

SHAKED   And this court is supposed to believe that you did not learn how to operate a diesel engine until two years after the war?

JOHN   It's the truth.

SHAKED   Have you ever killed a man Mr. Demjanjuk?

JOHN   No. I could not even kill a chicken. My wife did it.

SHAKED   But you fought in the Red Army. You never shot anyone?

JOHN   NO. The very idea made me sick.

Scene 18

FRAÜLEIN   John has another flashback. 1941.

ROSIE   Not a very good year to be a German, eh, Fraülein?

FRAÜLEIN   Shut up.

ROSIE   How do you bake a German chocolate cake?

FRAÜLEIN   Not now.

ROSIE   First you occupy ze kitchen. Ha! In the trenches. Desperation! Darkness! Flashes of light! The Soviets—

FRAÜLEIN   are pushed back by the Nazis. John and his comrade Mordecai are the only ones left in their unit...

MORDECAI   Look at it. The hills are crawling with Krauts. I can feel them crawling in my skin. I'd shoot myself if it wouldn't kill me. (*They laugh.*)

JOHN   All you talk about is shooting. I'm hungry.

MORDECAI   Well, we've got a quarter loaf of mouldy bread—

JOHN   Ssssh! I think I hear someone.

MORDECAI   Let 'em hear. Maybe they'll have something for us to eat. Maybe we'll shoot 'em and roast them. Human flesh. Tastes like pork but it's kosher.

JOHN   Quiet.... Mordecai, you're not right in the head.

MORDECAI   This is it, John. There's no rules. It might be a war, but we can do whatever the hell we want. (*hinting*) There were a couple of hungry 16-year-old girls in the village back there.

JOHN   I liked the redhead.

MORDECAI   Oh. You're not such a mama's boy after all. Here. Take my gun.

JOHN   What am I shooting?

MORDECAI   Me.

JOHN   I don't want to kill you.

MORDECAI   You're not gonna kill me. (*puts bread on his head*) Target practice.

JOHN   You know I'm not a good shot.

MORDECAI   So you better practice up.

JOHN   What if I kill you?

MORDECAI   What's another dead Jew?

JOHN   Oh stop. We've known each other since we were kids.

MORDECAI   Yeah. And you're an anti-Semite. Like all Ukes.

JOHN   Look, it's not my fault you killed Christ.

MORDECAI   I didn't kill Christ. My uncle Lazer did it. (*They laugh.*)

JOHN   The priest once said you use Christian blood to make matzoh.

MORDECAI   It's true. Those little Christian boys make the best matzoh. (*MORDECAI puts bread back on his head.*) Come on. Shoot me. This is your chance to get even. Stupid peasant.

> *JOHN shoots. Gun is empty. They laugh.*

SCENE 19

Enter NAZI 1 and NAZI 2

NAZI 1   *Halts maul!* Drop ze gun!

NAZI 2   DON'T MOVE!

NAZI 1   We've been listening.

NAZI 2   We couldn't see you.

NAZI 1   Idiots.

NAZI 2   Fools.

NAZI 1 & NAZI 2   Ha ha ha ha ha!

NAZI 2   Shut up.

NAZI 1   Shut up.

NAZI 2   Shut up!

NAZI 1 & NAZI 2   Ha ha ha ha ha!

NAZI 1   I want to kill them.

NAZI 2   I want to squeeze them.

NAZI 1   Little Russian Teddy bears.

NAZI 2   Little bears.

NAZI 1   Kill them.

NAZI 2   Can't.

NAZI 1   Kill them!

NAZI 2   CAN'T. Remember our orders.

NAZI 1   Remember Nietzsche. Or Goethe.

NAZI 2   Or Sven, the great herring merchant from Bremen:

NAZI 1   Everything German is Great!

NAZI 1 & NAZI 2   *Sieg heil!*

NAZI 2   Okay. We kill one. Keep the other.

NAZI 1   *Jah.* Which one of you was talking about roasting krauts?

   A beat. No one says anything. NAZI 1 and NAZI 2 become menacing.

NAZI 2   Is no one

NAZI 1   Talking?

NAZI 2   Are you two

NAZI 1   Friends?

Pause.

JOHN   He was, sir.

NAZI 1 kills MORDECAI.

NAZI 2   Oh. *Gott im Himmel.* Maybe that was the wrong one.

NAZI 1 & NAZI 2   Hahahahahaha!

NAZI 1   Shut up!

NAZI 2   Shut up!

NAZI 1   Shut up!

JOHN   If it pleases you, sir, he was a Jew.

NAZI 1 & NAZI 2   Jew?

JOHN   Yessirs.

NAZI 2   Well. Then justice has clearly been done.

NAZI 1   Once again, Divine Providence is *mit ze* German people.

NAZI 2   *Heil* Hitler!

NAZI 1   *Deutschland über alles!* (*a beat*)

NAZI 2   You're fairly strong, I see.

NAZI 1   Well-built.

NAZI 2   You have blue eyes—

JOHN   They're green, actually—

NAZI 1 & NAZI 2   Blue!

NAZI 2   There's something very

NAZI 1   Aryan about you.

NAZI 2   Can you drive a truck?

JOHN   Yes.

NAZI 2   Good *mit* engines?

JOHN   Yes.

NAZI 1   *Sehr gut.* (*a beat*)

NAZI 2   Why don't you join our club?

JOHN   No.

NAZI 1   Well there is another way out, you know.

NAZI 2   Yes, through the chimney.

NAZI 1 & NAZI 2   Hahahahahahaha.

NAZI 1   Membership you will find

NAZI 2   Has its privileges…

> *NAZI 2 imprints tattoo under JOHN's arm.*

SCENE 20

FRAÜLEIN   Back in court, Shaked further tightens his grip. John begins to *shvitz*.

SHAKED   Why did you remove your tattoo in 1945?

JOHN   Because I found out it identified me as an SS soldier.

SHAKED   So you were SS?

JOHN   No. The tattoo indicated my blood type.

SHAKED   Then why remove it?

JOHN   I was afraid it might be taken the wrong way.

SHAKED   And how did you come by your tattoo?

JOHN   At a certain point as a prisoner I was made to be a soldier.

SHAKED   What year?

JOHN   1944.

SHAKED   By the Nazis?

JOHN   Yes. A Ukranian auxiliary. Vlassov's army. We were all given tattoos but different from those of the SS.

SHAKED   You just said they were the same.

JOHN   They were similar.

SHAKED   What did you do in this auxiliary?

JOHN   I guarded military personnel.

SHAKED   Did you choose to be a soldier for the Nazis?

JOHN   No, I was ordered to.

SHAKED   The years 1942-43 you claim you were a POW in Chelm.

JOHN   Yes.

SHAKED   Describe to the court what it was like.

JOHN   The Nazis would beat us constantly. I was starving. I would've done anything for a piece of bread.

SHAKED   Really? How long were you in Chelm for?

JOHN   Eighteen months.

SHAKED   Can you tell me any of the names of the other prisoners?

JOHN   No. But their faces are clear to me.

SHAKED   Mr. Demjanjuk, you claim you spent most of the second world war as a POW in Chelm.

JOHN   Yes.

SHAKED   And it was an atrocity you can't forget, just as you can't forget the famine in Ukraine.

JOHN   These are atrocities that I want to forget, but can't, just as anyone who survived the Holocaust.

SHAKED   So when you were first indicted in 1978 these details were still fresh in your mind?

JOHN   Yes.

SHAKED   But in 1978 you never mentioned Chelm.

JOHN   Because it didn't come to mind then.

SHAKED   You spent a year and a half in Chelm.

JOHN   I can't help what I forget.

SHAKED   Your alibi is Chelm, Mr. Demjanjuk. Do you understand what that means?

JOHN   Yes.

SHAKED   And yet there is not a single witness to support this claim. And your testimony is vague and contradictory.

JOHN   I am answering in this manner because no one prepared me the way they prepare witnesses in Israel to give replies.

SHAKED   Mr. Demjanjuk—

JOHN   My only mistake is I can't think properly and I don't know how to answer accordingly.

SHAKED   You don't need to be prepared to tell the truth.

Scene 21

In the cell. JOHN is alone.

JOHN   But I was in Chelm.
So what if I can't remember their names?
I don't even remember the names of people I met last week.

I live in America.
I work, eat, spend time with my family.
I sleep well.
I'm a good man.

IVAN appears.

IVAN   As remarkable as a diesel engine.

JOHN   No. Practical.

IVAN   1941.

JOHN   I was starving in the mud flats of the Steppe.

IVAN   1942.

JOHN   I was a ghost in the forests of Poland.

IVAN   1943.

JOHN   I... don't remember.

IVAN   Really? How is it you haven't broken? Do you put your memories in a compartment and just forget? I can't. Killing was so easy back then. The hard part was how to dispose of the bodies. (*pause*)

At first we just threw them into ditches with some lime. But after a few months the smell was unbearable. Sometimes the earth would breathe. Geysers erupted when we walked the camp. Someone had the idea to burn them. But how does one burn one hundred thousand bodies? First you put the women on the bottom. Then the children. Then you attach the railroad ties. The men go on next. And then you light your match.

JOHN   Please.

IVAN   The motor of a tractor that sows the land that grows the crops
The motor of a tractor that runs and runs and never stops
The gasps the wails
The songs and tales
O, I can never forget those

Diesel. Thank God we switched to diesel. (*pause*) The worst was when the engine would break down, and the room was still full... The wails human beings can emit. Like dogs. Only worse.

JOHN   I was never near a gas chamber.

IVAN   Well let's go. Every man should see it. At least once.

ROSIE   Or twice.

IVAN   Fraülein, *musik, bitteschön!*

SCENE 22

Ukrainian music.

FRAÜLEIN   Step right up, step right up. Welcome to the Treblinka
Death Camp! Men, women, children. Everyone is welcome.
Admission is free.

IVAN   (*singing*) Can you hear the music
the prisoners play?
It's got a good reprise
today's a good day

I like their jazz
their kick and their swing
Here in Treblinka
they've got everything

There's vodka to drink
and whores in the village
So many benefits
who needs to rape and pillage

Ah, it's a good day for work
isn't it
isn't it

It's a good day to work
yes it is
Oh how I like it very much
running my engine in the sun

> *IVAN continues to take JOHN on a tour through the camp. IVAN
> and THE SURVIVOR play a sadistic game.*

IVAN   Main Exports, 1943

IVAN	**THE SURVIVOR**
suitcases	372 freight cars
bedding, down quilts, feathers	260 freight cars
men's suits	248 freight cars

religious artifacts	122 freight cars
hair compressed in bales	25 freight cars
miscellaneous items	400 freight cars

IVAN trips up THE SURVIVOR.

IVAN   A strong body. A strong mind. A strong spirit.

An artist must always
push himself.
I understood those children.
Their tears, like my art,
longed for the great audience.

I don't know why I asked
to have them thrown into the air.
Did Goethe control the words
that flew from his hands?

It was a mother's rain.
You should have seen
the waxed glint
on the babies' heads.

My blade
    blazing
beneath the lights

IVAN   *Achtung!* How would you say life is here?

THE SURVIVOR   Well the guards are very hospitable. They let us eat, for starters. Not much mind you, but they let us eat.

IVAN   How do you spend your days?

THE SURVIVOR   If I'm not hauling corpses, I'm playing in Arthur Gold's orchestra getting the prisoners excited for their imminent deaths.

IVAN   Isn't there any off time?

THE SURVIVOR   Certainly. The officers encourage us to fuck and
fall in love. It seems to amuse them, the possibility of love. And
on Yom Kippur they bring us succulent roast pig and Belgian
endive salad.

IVAN   I like Belgian endive salad. Do you?

JOHN   *No.*

IVAN   *(aside)* A mahogany pipe,
a gift from my dead father.
Smoke reflected
in my sword's blade.

Too distant to hear.

The shower of bodies falling,
night swallowing day.

Almost silence.

The ashes, the light,
these small bones.

I smoke my pipe.
Wanting peace.

SCENE 23

"The Ballad of John Demjanjuk Part II"

FRAÜLEIN   Now the years went by
and the war was long past
John raised a family
in Cleveland at last

He had what he wanted
the American dream
A job at Ford factory

SHEFTEL   Is that so obscene?

THE SURVIVOR   1976
    the place was New York
    We the survivors
    read the report

SHAKED   They looked at his picture
    they were sure it was him
    The man who had tortured them
    at every whim

SHEFTEL   The photos were biased
    the survivors confused
    No wonder they all said
    he's the gasser of Jews!

Scene 24

FRAÜLEIN   Now to the stand, the prosecution calls the survivor
    from Treblinka death camp—

THE SURVIVOR   I used to carry the bodies from the showers
    Sometimes I'd hide and
    nap beneath the incinerators
    The fumes left me with
    a bad eye and throat

    When Ivan made me lie with a corpse
    I had no choice
    I knew what he wanted me to do
    Nobody ordered him to do that

    You wonder how I can remember this man so well?

    (to JOHN) The night of the rebellion
    I made off with your eyes
    Stitched them into the wallet
    of my skin

Forty-four years I've carried
this ashen currency

*A thousand curses
unto you*, Ivan of Treblinka

May you hang from the olive tree and weep

Scene 25

FRAÜLEIN   Isn't barbed wire pretty?
    The way sunset
    can turn a fence
    to purple and gold?

    The end of the War! A Displaced Persons camp in Southern
    Germany. Behold the ruins that remain. And the love that grows
    from them.

    "Love in the DP Camp"

    (*singing*) The barbed wire was sparkling
    and the angels were calling
    That was the night John and Vera consummated their love

ROSIE   A new alibi John was trying
    So on the forms he kept lying
    John was afraid of being sent back to the Soviets

FRAÜLEIN   Now John wasn't alone
    The lovers longed for a home

ROSIE   They dreamed of a place in the States

FRAÜLEIN   He worked hard in the camp
    It was cold it was damp

ROSIE   He gave Vera the food on his plate

FRAÜLEIN   Yes the barbed wire was sparkling

ROSIE   And the angels were calling

CHORUS   That's when he popped that old question
And married her

JOHN   Under the fence

SCENE 26

IVAN and JOHN in the cell.

IVAN   Are you lonely?

JOHN   I've been alone for two years in this cell.

IVAN   So you're happy we're together.

JOHN   No.

IVAN   That's right. Vanichka doesn't get happy. Always working.
Trying to make the American dream. Only now there's no work to
do. So what does he do to pass the time?

JOHN   I write letters to my family. To Vera.

IVAN   Nice. I'm curious. How do you two like to fuck?

JOHN   Shut up.

IVAN   I prefer it from behind. Like a dog.

JOHN   Kurva.

IVAN   You like to talk while you do it?
Are you tender?
Or do you like to throw her against the wall—

JOHN   You're disgusting.

IVAN   Don't be so innocent. You used to talk like this with the boys when you were in Vlassov's army.

JOHN   I never talked about my wife in this way.

IVAN   Poles, Jews, Germans. All those women. They didn't even have time to say yes or no, did they? Sluts.

JOHN   I never raped.

IVAN   Oh no. The best thing about war crimes is when you're doing them, they're not crimes. Words like "rape" don't enter your mind. You're just "making love." The hard part is afterwards.

JOHN   I raised a family.

IVAN   So did I.

JOHN   I live for my family.

IVAN   You say that as though you could be sure of who you are.

JOHN   I am.

IVAN nods to FRAÜLEIN.

SCENE 27

"Two Faces are Better than One"

FRAÜLEIN   Oh yes it's true
a good possibility
That a man is a man
with many personalities
But can two faces
be one?

Well you know two faces
are better than one

You take your chances
you play your hand
The cards are shuffled
where do you stand?

You take your chances
You have your fun
But are two faces
just one?

It's not so easy
we all know
Being more than one person
can be very hard on the soul

A man is a killer
A man loves a lot
Is this the same man
what proof do we got?

Friedrich Nietzsche
did he have it right?
Are we doomed to our past
no matter how hard we're gonna fight?

People change
so some experts say
A man can forget
what he did yesterday

A face is different
or stays the same
Is it the same man
if a photo's all that remains?

So from your past John
you cannot run

If two faces
are one

SCENE 28

FRAÜLEIN   The Travniki card
Is an SS card
It has a photo of John

The Travniki card
Is it an authentic card?
Sheftel prays that it is wrong

In chambers.

SHEFTEL   The Travniki document is a forgery.

SHAKED   Prove it.

SHEFTEL   The signature is completely unlike that of my client's.

SHAKED   Then why did John admit it was "the way he wrote his name"?

SHEFTEL   The card says he was at Sobibor.

SHAKED   And Sobibor is 130 km from Treblinka.

SHEFTEL   The KGB supplied the card to this court.

SHAKED   They have the documents—

SHEFTEL   and they want John dead.

SHAKED   John himself admitted the picture resembles him.

SHEFTEL   He was confused by the question. I know this card's a forgery.

SHAKED   Such a good forgery nobody can tell that it's fake?

SHEFTEL   You're a self-righteous, Talmudic hair-splitting asshole.

SHAKED   You're an opportunistic *mamzer*, feeding off the desperation of the Ukrainian community.

SHEFTEL   I am going to demolish, shred this document to pieces, until there is nothing left.

FRAÜLEIN   *Bitte.* I hope he leaves us a little for the trial.

SHAKED   *(to the court)* The Prosecution would like to submit as evidence a 1942 paperclip. On this I.D. card there are rust marks left by a paperclip. If the rust mark is authentic, the card must be too. And John trained to be an SS guard at Travniki.

SHEFTEL   Is this card forged?

SHAKED   Or is it real?

FRAÜLEIN   The court must decide.

        Item #2641.
        John's life held
        by a paperclip

SHAKED   Fraülein. *Bitte.*

        FRAÜLEIN becomes the paperclip.

THE PAPERCLIP   I am the paperclip
        That might have held
        the picture
        of John to this card

        I am really a 1942 German
        paperclip
        Yes, evidence is
        getting hard

If I turn rusty
then the card
is true
the evidence in my lips

But no one's sure
if there was rust on
German-made
paperclips

So submit me for evidence
Hand me past the weak defence
I will make John hang
or set him free

His life is a paperclip
Trying to keep things
in one place

Oh, but it's loose
Things don't hold
Order turns to disgrace...

SCENE 29

Voices whisper:

VOICE 1   *Never cursed*
VOICE 2   *Never angry*
VOICE 3   *Never talked about the war*
VOICE 4   *He's the kinda guy who'd fix your bike*
IVAN   *even if you didn't really know him*
ALL   *And his perogies were...*

JOHN JR.   Dad?

JOHN   Junior.

JOHN JR.   What did you do during the war?

JOHN   Nothing.

JOHN JR.   Is that why you never talked about it?

> *JOHN moves toward JOHN JR. They start to bring their hands together. Just before they touch, the lights go out on JOHN JR.*

SCENE 30

IVAN   I have a gift for you.
A field. It was dark.
The earth was hard.
The moonlight fell on this in a particular way.
As though the moon were pointing, *here you are, here you are...*

Sleep, old friend. Sleep.

SCENE 31

"Time Passes Slowly"

> *While singing, IVAN reveals a baby shoe and puts it in the pocket of JOHN, who is sleeping.*

ROSIE   Time passes slowly
with the drip drip drabble
Listening to the holy
cell wall rabble

IVAN   Let the dark
leave its mark

Twelve years waiting
while the world is spinning

memories forgotten,
now reappear

ROSIE   Time passes slowly
   with the drip drip drabble
   He's listening to the holy
   cell wall rabble

Scene 32

FRAÜLEIN   Trial day three-hundred and ninety-five. What goes
  on in the boys' room? Our two handsome lawyers, Shaked and
  Sheftel, get close and personal at the urinals.

SHAKED   Sheffie.

SHEFTEL   Mickey.

   An awkward piss.

SHAKED   Report's back. There was rust on the paperclip.

SHEFTEL   Of course. You forge that too? *(a beat)* I saw Mike
  Wallace up in the balcony.

SHAKED   "Sixty Minutes" is doing a special.

SHEFTEL   There's no business like Shoah business.

SHAKED   Tell that to the survivors.

SHEFTEL   Sentimental prick.

SHAKED   I can't wait to see you lose in front of the entire world.

SHEFTEL   I don't lose anything I take on.

SHAKED   Your client's not doing too well out there.

SHEFTEL   My client's a stupid goy. He's too dumb to have killed
  a million people.

SHAKED   Glad to see you respect your client.

SHEFTEL   I want you to know: I've got a lead that could destroy
you.

SHAKED   You're bluffing.

SHEFTEL   Am I? I don't want a plea bargain. Even if you offered it
to me.

SHAKED   What's this lead?

SHEFTEL   You think I'm gonna tell you?

SHAKED   What you know could be in both our interests. That is, if
you actually care about the truth.

SHEFTEL   Whose truth? I'm the only person in this damned
country who wants to find out what this man actually did during
the war.

Scene 33

FRAÜLEIN   Trial records page eight thousand and sixty-five. Back
in court, the defense calls the Survivor from Treblinka death camp
to the stand. Again.

SHEFTEL   (*places a book down on the stand*) Sir, is this your
handwriting?

THE SURVIVOR   Yes.

SHEFTEL   Do you remember when you wrote this?

THE SURVIVOR   1945.

SHEFTEL   Would you say that what you wrote was a true account
of life in Treblinka?

THE SURVIVOR   Yes.

SHEFTEL   Is it true that the night of the Treblinka uprising you saw Ivan the Terrible killed in the gas chamber?

THE SURVIVOR   No.

SHEFTEL   But you wrote it in your account.

THE SURVIVOR   I wrote what I was told.

SHEFTEL   You wrote that you saw him killed.

THE SURVIVOR   It was the others who told me.

SHEFTEL   You wrote, right here, that you saw Ivan the Terrible killed with a shovel.

THE SURVIVOR   I wanted to believe that. That was our dream.

SHEFTEL   Then why did you not point out the difference between what you wrote and what you saw?

THE SURVIVOR   I wish I had been there. *(pointing to JOHN)* If I had been there, he would not be sitting across from me. Wipe that grin from your face!

> *JOHN starts to laugh. THE SURVIVOR walks over to JOHN. JOHN rises.*

JOHN   Atah Shakran!

THE SURVIVOR   Don't you call me a liar.

SCENE 34

Courtroom freezes.

JOHN   Did you see that? The Survivor's made a fool of himself.

IVAN   This is Israel. They're going to hang you. Even if you're not Ivan.

JOHN   I AM NOT IVAN. You were killed.

IVAN   Maybe I was. Maybe I wasn't.

JOHN   I will not die for something I didn't do.

IVAN   And what did you do, John?

JOHN   I don't remember the details.

IVAN   You don't want to remember.

JOHN   I thought you were going to help me.

IVAN   I already have.

JOHN   Where are you going ?

IVAN   To the Western Wall. I like to watch the Jews pray. Their songs bring me a certain peace.

IVAN whispers into THE SURVIVOR's ear, "Attah Shakran."

SCENE 35

Unfreeze.

THE SURVIVOR   Don't you call me a liar…

FRAÜLEIN   Order in the Court! Order in the court!

SHEFTEL   Your Honour, I need a short recess. John? What the hell was that about?

JOHN   I can't do it.

SHEFTEL   Just take a deep breath. Everything will be fine. We're winning. It's your final statement. Relax.

JOHN   I can't think straight—

SHEFTEL   John, grab a hold of yourself.

JOHN   Not guilty. Guilty.

SHEFTEL   Jesus, John.

JOHN   What if I was a guard.

SHEFTEL   What?

JOHN   *(pause)* At a camp.

SHEFTEL   *(A beat. SHEFTEL is taken aback. He recovers.)* That's not what you're on trial for. The rules were different during the war. Maybe you did some wrong things back then. But not genocide.

JOHN   Yoram. Am I a good man?

SHEFTEL   You're a survivor, John.

JOHN   Yes. I am.

SHEFTEL   Now get up there and make your final statement. I will not lose this case.

SCENE 36

Back in court.

JOHN   I'm a simple man
with a simple mind.
I have no knowledge of
systems and laws.

I live in America
with my family.
I have a vegetable garden.
When I sink my hands into the earth
I feel peace,
moist and soft,
something to grab onto.

You've been watching me for twelve years now.
You're watching to see
what I have seen.
It's these hands that have seen a lot.
Motors and children
harvests and perogies.
These hands have seen the ocean,
embraced love,
filled out forms—

People of Israel, I need you
to understand. I am not Ivan of Treblinka.
I learned the order of the engine
so I could survive.

I breathed
hot metal,
the sparks from a torch,
bodies of automobiles
cooling on the line.
Ten hours a day
five days a week
for twenty-five years…

Thank God for America,
I remind myself each day.
Thank God for America.

SCENE 37

FRAÜLEIN   April, 1988. The day of the Verdict has arrived. The doors to the courtroom open at eight a.m., but the first spectators have lined up since midnight. When the police van arrives at the court, John refuses to get out. A sound emits from his mouth, a high-pitched whimper, like a dog. He must be carried into court by four guards. Kicking and screaming and crying.

The Court of Israel finds John Demjanjuk... guilty!

JOHN   *(speaking)* My Vera faints.
Junior weeps. The Jewish students chant.

VOICES   Am Yisrael Chai, Am Yisrael Chai!

JOHN   An eye for an eye.
A tooth for a tooth.

SCENE 38

IVAN   Soon they'll put that noose around your neck
and you'll be sweating
and the people chanting
blood, blood, we have his blood—

JOHN   I'm not dead yet.

IVAN   No.

JOHN   I still have hope.

IVAN   Really. Why?

JOHN   I don't know. Maybe that's how I survive.

SCENE 39

FRAÜLEIN   So you think it's over for John?

ROSIE   Yes!

FRAÜLEIN   No way. Sheftel's appeal races forward like a white Porsche on the Autobahn.

ROSIE   John sits on death row for four years.

FRAÜLEIN   Sheftel is persistent

ROSIE   Sheftel won't quit.

SHEFTEL   I would like to submit as evidence, a telegram from the KGB to the OSI.

Dear Sirs: Your request to identify John Demjanjuk as Ivan the Terrible has turned out negative.
Eighty accounts from thirty former Treblinka guards name Marchenko as Ivan.
John Demjanjuk never at Treblinka.
Date of telegram:
April, 1978.

Ladies and gentlemen. Fifteen years ago today there was evidence that would have acquitted my client in any standard court of law. Why the U.S. and Israeli governments chose to suppress this information we can only imagine.

Christine Brubaker
photo by Jonathan Garfinkel

SCENE 40

FRAÜLEIN   All rise in the court of law!
The Supreme Court of Israel rules
that John Demjanjuk
is not Ivan of Treblinka.

The verdict overturned. The appeal won.

JOHN   (*singing*) Tonight I dream of home in Ohio
The lawn smells like the sun
and the trees
shush golden in the breeze
Cries of children
ice cream trucks
and my face
full of sun
Summer on my skin
at last

FRAÜLEIN   John returns to his loving family in America.
But at a Cleveland Indians' baseball game...

JOHN   It's all over now.

IVAN   Over? They picket on your lawn.

ROSIE   *Murderer.*

IVAN   Wear gold stars.

ROSIE   *Ivan the Terrible.*

IVAN   But you got away with it.

JOHN   Justice was served.

IVAN   Congratulations. Let's have a hot dog.

JOHN   I don't want a hot dog. I'd like to just enjoy the game.

IVAN   Who's winning?

JOHN   We are.

IVAN   The U.S. is reopening your naturalization file, Vanishka. Your trials aren't over.

Scene 41

IVAN   1941.

VOICES   *1941*

JOHN   I was starving in the mud flats of the Steppe.

IVAN   1942.

VOICES   *1942*

JOHN   I was a ghost in the forests of Poland.

IVAN   1943…

VOICES   *1943*

    Flashback, 1943.

JOHN   I'm in the field.

IVAN   The sky is black.

JOHN   The trees are listening.

IVAN   There's only a few of them.

JOHN   And I don't even have to dig their grave.

IVAN   All you have to do is pull the trigger.

Dmitry Chepovetsky, Frank Moore
photo by Jonathan Garfinkel

JOHN   All they have to do is gather themselves and kill me.

IVAN   They won't.

JOHN   There's a girl in a white skirt.

IVAN   That's the girl I'm gonna have.

JOHN   There's a man praying.
His passion rises toward me.

IVAN   His passion is mine.

JOHN   Life

IVAN   or death.

JOHN   I wish I could drop my gun and run.

IVAN   The choice is yours.

JOHN   I wish that one didn't look like my mother.
I want to run back to Ukraine.

IVAN   Not even the moon is innocent.

JOHN   A woman breastfeeds her child.
The child wipes its mouth,
there's too much milk,
the skin is so white

IVAN   I want to drink it!

JOHN pulls out the baby shoe from his pocket.

JOHN   The child drops its shoe.

IVAN   No bigger than my finger.

JOHN   Criminals?

IVAN   We were gods.

JOHN looks at the shoe, then the gun in IVAN's hands. Blackout.

Epilogue

Out of the black, THE SURVIVOR enters.

THE SURVIVOR   This is the end
of our story tonight
But when I go to sleep
will things be all right?

What once was Treblinka
is now farm and grass
There are lupines and elm trees
where the slow train rolls past

But what's dead's not done
what's gone comes again
Good night my children,
my judges, my friends

Fin

Regular Fella

Garfinkel/Brubaker

THE MYTH OF IVAN THE TERRIBLE

GARFINKEL/COLE

Time Passes Slowly

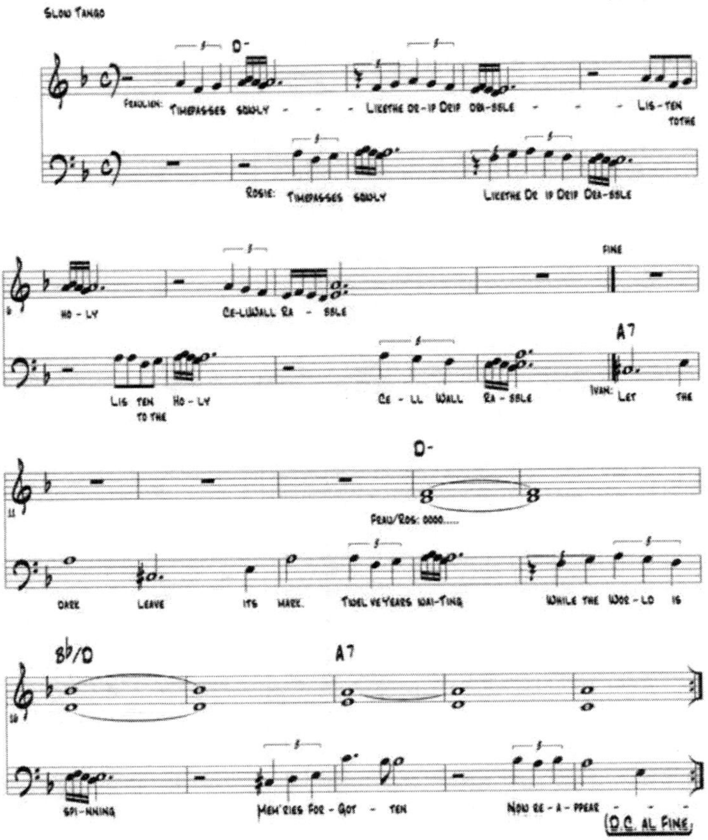

photo by Mindy Stricke

Jonathan Garfinkel is a poet and playwright. He is the author of the book of poetry *Glass Psalms* (Turnstone Press 2005), and the plays *Walking to Russia* (Playwrights Guild of Canada, 2002) and *The Trials of John Demjanjuk: A Holocaust Cabaret*. He is currently doing his Masters degree at University of Toronto in English Literature in the Field of Creative Writing.